Next Generation
Paper Airplanes

SAM ITA

Photography by Céline Ribordy

TUTTLE Publishing

Tokyo | Rutland, Vermont | Singapore

Contents

The Planes

The Basic 10

The Dart 12

The Bat 14

The Deco Dart 17

Introduction

One of my most vivid childhood memories is of a paper airplane contest held at the Kingdome in Seattle, Washington. The rules were simple; Several huge circles were painted on the floor of the arena. The names of prizes were spelled out in the circles. From the stands, thousands of contestants would throw airplanes, folded from sheets of paper with their names written on them. You had to buy the paper. At the end of the day, the pilot whose plane ended up closest to the center of the circle won the prize. A trip to Disney World was the grand prize. There was also a Jeep parked on the floor with its windows open. The first person to get a plane inside won the vehicle. Serious contestants purchased stacks of paper and brought homemade launchers, staples, rolls of tape, bone folders, etc.

My family and I, on the other hand, were woefully ill-prepared. We had traveled across the country to visit my grandmother, and were attending the contest on a whim. This was the mid 1980s. I had mastered shoe tying not too long before. In any case, the designated paper cost 25¢ per sheet, so we only bought about a half dozen. Folding instructions for "The Dart" (page 12) were printed on each sheet.

I vaguely recall a couple of attempts. My darts began their descent, just after leaving my hand, landing just a few rows in front of our seats. My parents hadn't fared much better. Their adult strength enabled them to throw their darts only another ten or twenty rows. None of my family's aircraft even made it out of the stands. I now blame this poor performance on The Dart's major design flaws. I will get into this subject more later.

For the purpose of this book, darts are an entire category of paper plane. They are long, pointy, and built for going the distance—the sort of plane that should have been ideal for this contest. With decent folding, a good throw, and a little luck, I believed any of my darts could have made it to the Kingdome's floor.

Although it would have been nice to have done better in the contest, what I remember most about the contest was how incredibly fun it was, and how I've always wanted a chance to try it again. The contest was held annually from 1978 to 1987. I have never heard of anything quite like it, since. The Kingdome was demolished in 2000.

In the same spirit, I designed these planes for maximum enjoyment. They represent a variety of forms and flight styles. For the most part, they require only beginner level origami skills. There are a few intermediate-level folds, which are explained in detail. If you get stuck, just pop in the DVD, so you can watch the process on your television or computer. Happy flying!

Folding Instructions

Naturally, you want to skip the instructions and jump right into folding the planes. I can't blame you, but I should mention that if you are a beginner, these instructions can save you much confusion and frustration. I made this mistake for many years. I would have become a better folder, much faster, had I not.

Dashed lines indicate **Valley Folds**. This means that the crease ends up at the bottom of the completed fold. The arrow indicates the direction that the paper should be folded.

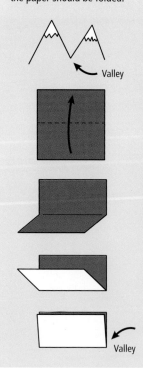

Mountain Folds go the other way. They are represented by a line of dots and dashes, or sometimes just dots. This means that the crease ends up on top, once the fold is complete. I think of the dots as peaks of mountains.

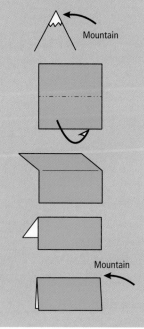

A double headed arrow means you need to fold and unfold. This weakens the paper slightly, leaving a crease.

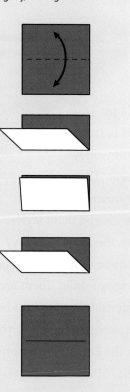

The **Squash Fold** is very common in origami and paper planes.

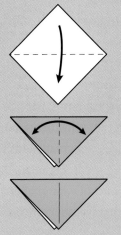

The **Outlined Arrow** means "push." It is telling you to apply pressure to the paper, along a given direction. In this case, it refolds a previous valley fold, while creating two new mountain folds.

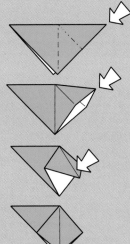

The completed **Squash Fold**.

The **Inside Reverse Fold** is also very common.

It usually follows a crease, created by a previous fold and unfold.

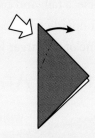

Now, push against the center, creating mountain folds on both sides.

The completed **Inside Reverse Fold**.

The **Pivot Fold** involves moving a flap of paper around a set point, then re-squashing in another position. This fold begins where the previous one left off.

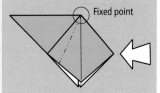

Fixed point

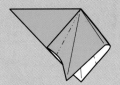

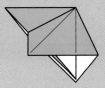

The completed **Pivot Fold**.

Paper in Flight

Paper airplanes and kites were the first man-made objects to take flight. Unfortunately, they are fragile, and tend not to survive as artifacts, leaving paper airplane history rather lacking. Interestingly, the Wright brothers used paper planes to test their theories of flight. Thankfully, we now know a great deal about mechanical flight, whereas many aspects of paper glider flight remain, to a degree, mysterious. Commercial aircraft routinely fly through rainstorms, but slight details, such as humidity or invisible folding differences can greatly affect a paper plane's ability to fly. Of course, a tailwind can make a mediocre plane fly great. Dealing with these random, unpredictable factors is part of what makes paper planes fun. Let's focus on some of the larger factors that we can control.

Paper Aircraft Anatomy

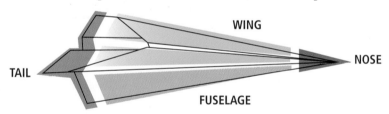

WING

NOSE

TAIL

FUSELAGE

PRIMARY FORCES

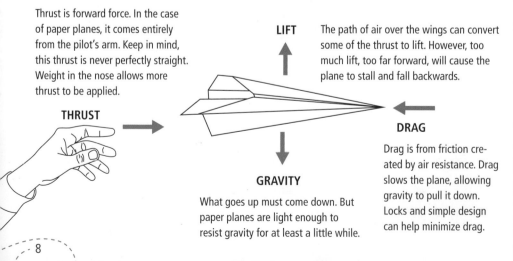

Thrust is forward force. In the case of paper planes, it comes entirely from the pilot's arm. Keep in mind, this thrust is never perfectly straight. Weight in the nose allows more thrust to be applied.

THRUST

LIFT

The path of air over the wings can convert some of the thrust to lift. However, too much lift, too far forward, will cause the plane to stall and fall backwards.

DRAG

Drag is from friction created by air resistance. Drag slows the plane, allowing gravity to pull it down. Locks and simple design can help minimize drag.

GRAVITY

What goes up must come down. But paper planes are light enough to resist gravity for at least a little while.

Cross Section View

If you were to look at a cross section of The Dart, it would look something like this. Notice, in the first diagram below, the fuselage is not locked, so it tends to hang wide open.

When the wings slope at a downward angle, like this, they are said to form a negative *dihedral*, or *anhedral*.

Wings at a negative dihedral can have a parachute effect, which helps the plane stay in the air. They tend to be unstable, though. Sometimes, they will even flip over.

Now, let's compare this to a straight-on view of the Deco Dart.

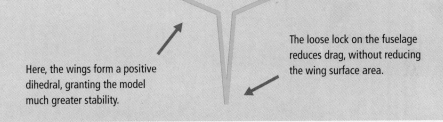

Here, the wings form a positive dihedral, granting the model much greater stability.

The loose lock on the fuselage reduces drag, without reducing the wing surface area.

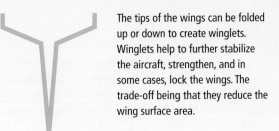

The tips of the wings can be folded up or down to create winglets. Winglets help to further stabilize the aircraft, strengthen, and in some cases, lock the wings. The trade-off being that they reduce the wing surface area.

The Basic

"The Basic" represents the ultimate lazy paper aircraft design. That said, with careful folding and proper adjustment, if launched indoors with all the windows closed, you should get a fraction of a second of nice flight before this plane stalls and tumbles to the floor. Most of the problem is its lack of weight in the front. The center of balance is way t oo far back.

Despite (or perhaps because of) its shortcomings, The Basic, with its tall fuselage and short wings, possesses a certain charm. If nothing else, it provides a clear demonstration of how paper interacts with the air around it. Its simple design leaves plenty of room for experimentation and improvement.

Orientation

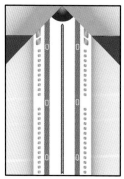

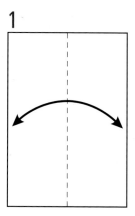

1

Begin with the printed side facing down, with the long sides oriented vertically. Valley fold through the center and unfold.

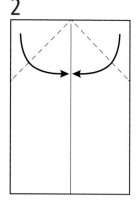

2

Fold the top edges to the central crease.

3

Refold the central valley fold.

Rotate 90 degrees.

4

Fold the front wing down.

5

Fold the rear wing down.

6

Level the wings and launch.

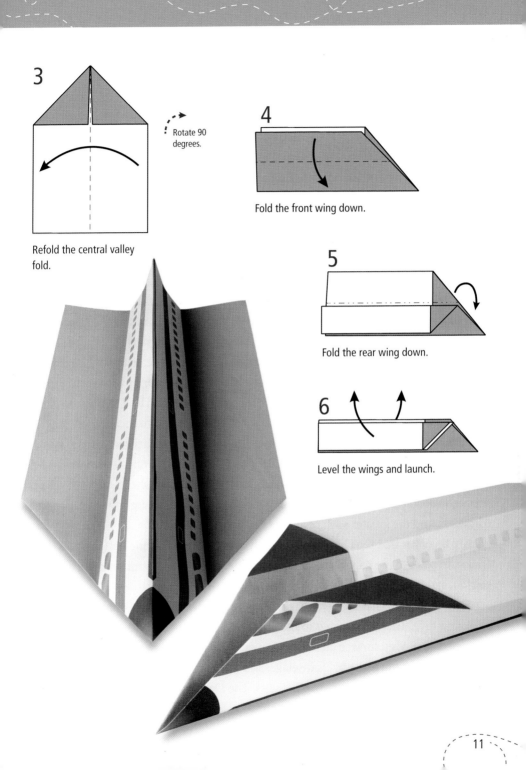

The Dart

When most of us think of paper airplanes, the first image that comes to mind is that of the Dart. You might picture a mischievous student throwing this plane into the math teacher's head. In reality, it would more likely begin its descent immediately after it left the student's hand, and slide across the floor to her feet.

So, why does the Dart fly so poorly?

Some argue that the nose is not heavy enough. They add paper-clips to increase the weight. I disagree with this approach. Sure, adding weight will help achieve a longer flight; but not due to better balance, stability, or lift. Rather, the additional weight simply allows you to exert greater force. I assert that once you begin adding materials, other than paper, you are no longer dealing with paper airplanes. You might as well throw rocks. Moreover, the nose is already twice folded over, and the center of gravity is quite far forward, considering that the wings are so narrow at nose.

Others blame the lack of a locking mechanism. They advocate taping the plane shut. True, the layers of folding make for a great deal of outward pressure, forcing the wings to a negative dihedral. In my experiments, I have found that taping the plane shut, or locking the back does reduce drag, but does nothing to increase lift or glide. On the contrary, the best flights I've achieved were from a rather loose, open plane, plane with increased wing surface. Still, the negative dihedral makes for inconsistent and unstable flights. I found that darts folded from larger sheets of paper fly a bit better, probably due to the folds holding together a little more tightly maintaining a dihedral, and the greater surface area of the wings.

My theory is that the Dart suffers mostly, from a more specific design flaw. The outward push of the paper, and the shape of the wings create something of a negative airfoil, causing the plane to sink.

So, I concluded that the Dart, the most iconic paper airplane, is simply designed to take a dive. Then it occurred to me; if I throw the plane upside down, its flaws are reversed. The wing surface increases. The negative dihedral becomes positive and stable. Holding the plane by its fuselage, and pitching it underhand at an upward angle makes for consistently strong flights. The Dart has been a great plane all along. We've just been throwing it upside down!

Orientation

1

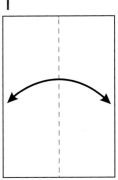

Begin with the printed side facing down, with the long sides oriented vertically. Valley fold through the center and unfold.

2

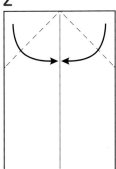

Fold the top edges to central crease.

3

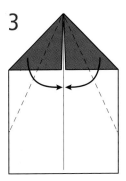

Again, valley fold the top edges to the central crease.

4

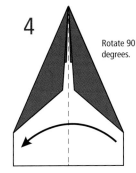

Rotate 90 degrees.

Fold top edges to center.

5

Fold the wings down.

6

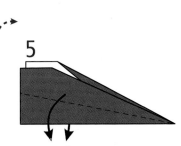

Turn over.

The result.

7

Grasp the model by the fuselage, and pitch it at an upward angle.

The Bat

This glider was designed around a lock in the very front, which happens to take the form of a bat's head, and locks the wings in place. Unlike a real bat, which darts around in the air, this plane has more of a gradual, floating flight style. It's a fun plane to fold from dark-colored paper. Practice this one, so you can fold a bunch for Halloween.

Orientation

1

Begin with printed side facing up, with the long side oriented horizontally. Valley fold through the center and unfold.

2

Turn over.

Fold the top edges to the central vertical crease.

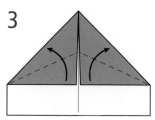

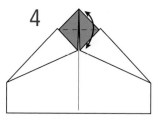

3

Valley fold the inside corners to the outside folded edges.

4

Valley fold and unfold the upper rhombus.

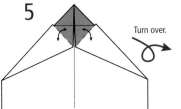

5

Fold and unfold to the center through all layers, along the bottom edges of the upper rhombus.

Turn over.

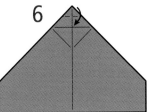

6

Valley fold the top corner to the crease.

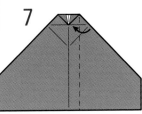

7

Valley fold the outer edge to meet the edge of the top triangle.

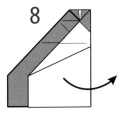

8

Unfold.

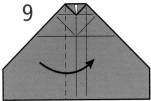

9

Valley fold the outer edge to meet the edge of the top triangle.

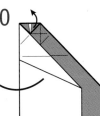

10

Unfold the wing and the top triangle.

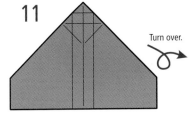

11

The result.

Turn over.

12

Valley fold all layers down along the bottom corner of the rhombus.

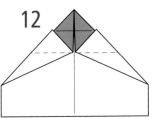

13

Push up the corner while folding along the central crease to form a rabbit ear.

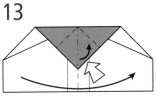

14

Step 13 in progress.

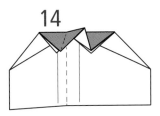

15

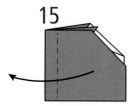

Valley fold the wing down, along the existing crease.

16

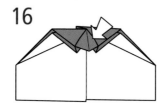

Squash fold to flatten the rabbit ear.

17

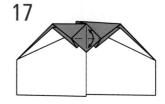

Fold the tip to the top, then unfold.

18

Mountain fold and tuck inside along the crease you just made.

19

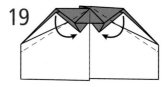

Valley fold the top edges, through all layers, as far as they will go, and tuck them under the head.

20

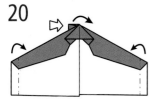

Fold the winglets downward, and straighten the fuselage.

21

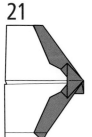

Set the dihedrals, shape the wings, and prepare for flight.

The Deco Dart

If I could go back in time, this is the plane I would have entered in that contest in the Kingdome. It's basically a dressed up, overachieving Dart. This design preserves the clean lines and profile of the Dart, while adding weight to the front and loosely locking the fuselage and wings for satisfying, consistent flights.

Don't be intimidated by the number of steps. With a little practice, you should be able to fold this model in a couple of minutes. Other than a couple of rabbit ears and squash folds, this is a very straightforward model to fold. I would enter it head to head in any sort of impromptu contest.

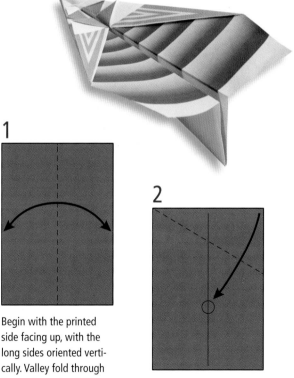

Orientation

1

Begin with the printed side facing up, with the long sides oriented vertically. Valley fold through the center and unfold.

2

Valley fold the top right corner to the central crease.

3

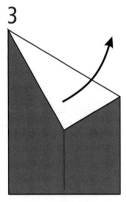

Unfold the previous step.

4

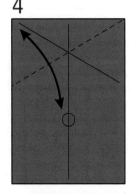

Repeat steps 2 and 3 on the left side.

5

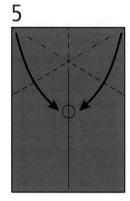

Collapse along the existing creases, forming a rabbit ear.

6

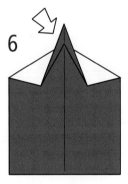

Continue to collapse and push flat.

7

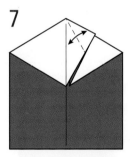

Fold the top edge to the central crease. Unfold.

8

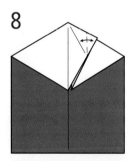

Fold the bottom edge to the crease created in the previous step. Unfold.

9

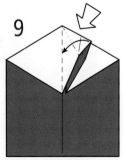

Open the center flap and squash fold it down to the center, along the existing crease.

10

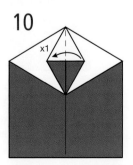

Valley fold one layer in half.

11

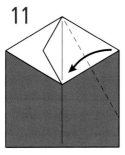

Valley fold the top edge
to the central crease.

12

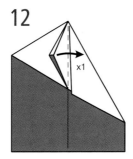

x1

Fold over one flap.

13

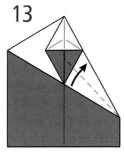

Valley fold the bottom
edge of the flap outward
to the edge.

14

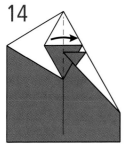

Fold the flap to the right.

15

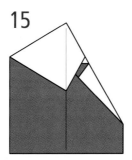

The result.

16

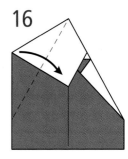

Valley fold the top edge to
the central crease.

17

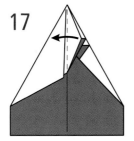

Fold over one flap.

18

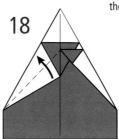

Fold the flap to the left.

19

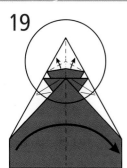

Fold the entire model in half and rabbit ear the uppermost triangle along the crease you made in step 8.

20

Pull the bottom of the top triangle as you fold the model in half.

21

The result.

22

Fold the wing down and squash fold to flatten the top triangle.

23

Flattening the top triangle in progress.

24

Level the wings and prepare for flight.

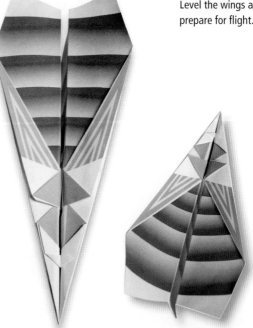

The Flying Leaf

This plane is my answer to "The Basic." As with my changes to "The Dart," I added weight to the nose and reinforced the wings. I like this one a lot. It is endlessly customizable, easy to fold, and the wings can be made bigger or smaller. I like to throw it hard with an exaggerated dihedral, and see what it does. Sometimes, it makes for a long, slow, elegant flight.

The Falling Leaf will not set any world records, but, if I were stranded on a deserted island and my only companion is a single, rectangular sheet of paper, this plane would be a good one to fold.

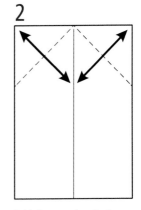

Orientation

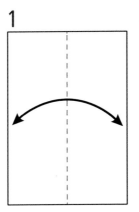

1

Begin with the printed side facing down, with the long sides oriented vertically. Valley fold through the center and unfold .

2

Fold the top edges to the central crease.

3

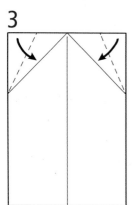

Valley fold the top edges to lie even with the creases you just made.

4

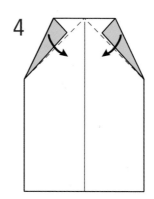

Valley fold along the existing creases.

5

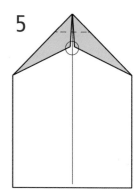

Valley fold the tip to the bottom of the folded edges.

6

Turn over.

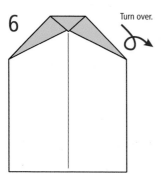

The result.

7

Rotate 90 degrees.

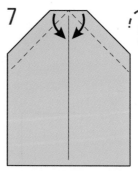

Valley fold the top edges to the central crease.

8

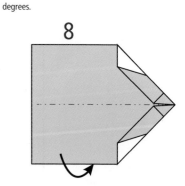

Mountain fold in half.

9

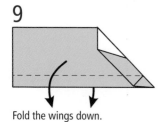

Fold the wings down.

10

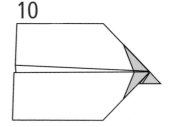

The completed Flying Leaf.

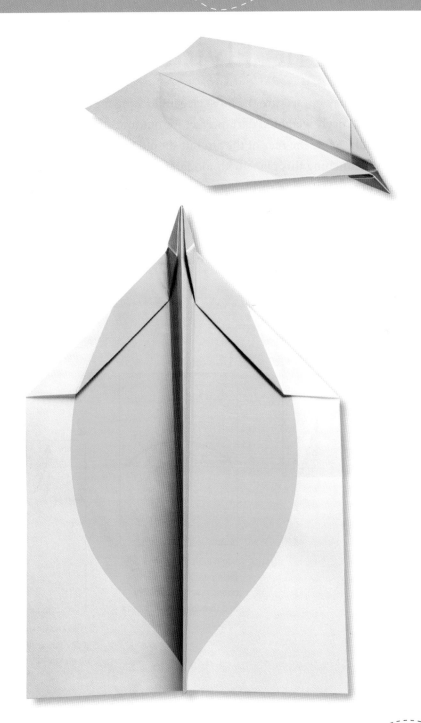

The Flying Turnip

This plane may not feature the most elegant locking mechanism, but it makes for a solid, nicely weighted dart, perfect for outdoor flight. The front should lock solidly, while the rear of the aircraft should be expected to hang open, loosely. Launching this plane with moderate force should provide a similar degree of satisfaction to throwing an actual turnip, but without having to worry about breaking any windows.

Orientation

1

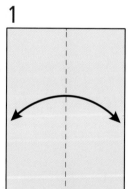

Begin with the printed side facing up, with long sides oriented vertically. Valley fold through the center and unfold.

2

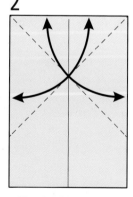

Fold and unfold the top edge to the side edges, making creases that form an X.

3

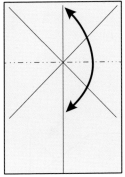

Mountain fold the top edge back, through the center of the X. Unfold.

4

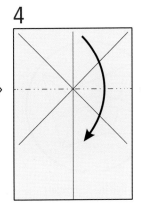

Push the sides of horizontal crease inward and forward to create mountain folds, while pulling the entire top forward and down.

5

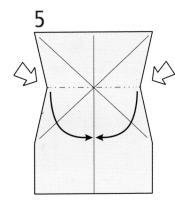

You are forming a "water bomb base." This form is very important in origami, and is the basis for many different paper airplanes.

6

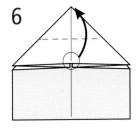

Valley fold the center of the bottom of the triangle to the tip. The model will not lay flat.

7

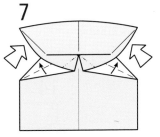

Valley fold the lower triangles in half, while pushing up and flattening the top of the model.

8

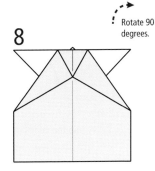

Rotate 90 degrees.

The result.

9

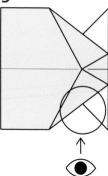

Pull up the triangular flap and look underneath.

10

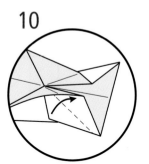

Valley fold the flap underneath in half.

11

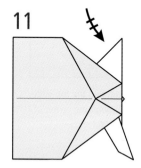

Repeat steps 9 and 10 on the other side.

12

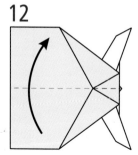

Valley fold the plane in half.

13

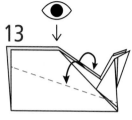

Valley fold the wings in half, and view from top.

14

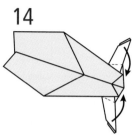

Valley fold the arms inward along the nose of the plane, crossing each other.

15

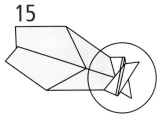

Zoom in on the nose.

16

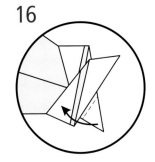

Valley fold the tip down along the edge.

17

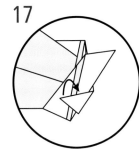

Tuck the tip under the lowest level.

18

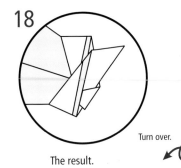

The result.

Turn over.

19

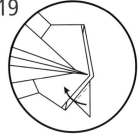

Valley fold the tip down along the edge.

20

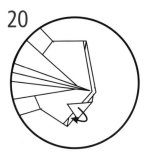

Tuck the tip under the lowest level.

21

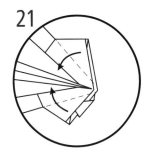

Valley fold the corners to the center along the front edges.

22

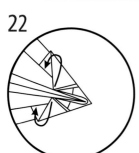

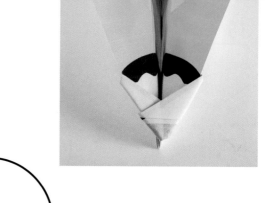

Tuck the corners under the lowest layers to complete the nose lock.

23

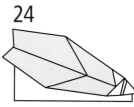

Turn the plane over and zoom out.

Turn over.

24

Level the wings and prepare for flight.

The Gremlin

The design of this plane was inspired by the AMC Gremlin, an American economy car from the 1970s. As with its namesake, this plane looks ugly, but it performs surprisingly well. A very fun model to fly and fold, it is sturdy enough to throw hard and suitable for outdoor flight.

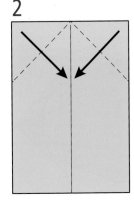

Orientation

1

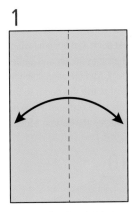

Begin with printed side facing up, with the long sides oriented vertically. Valley fold through the center and unfold.

2

Fold the top edges to the central crease.

3

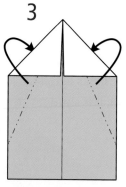

Mountain fold the top edges behind to the central crease, without creasing the top layer.

4

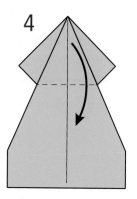

Make a valley fold at the narrowest point.

Turn over.

5

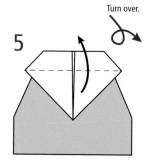

Valley fold the point up along a horizontal crease running between the two corners.

6

Rotate 90 degrees.

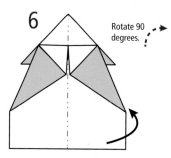

Mountain fold in half.

7

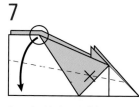

At point X, the model wing becomes thicker and harder to fold. Fold the wing down from just above this point, so that the front corner of the wing touches the bottom edge.

8

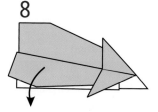

Pull the model open from the front wing.

9

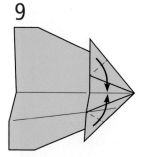

Valley fold the corners inward, as far as they will go.

10

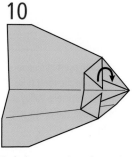

Tuck the corner into the pocket.

11

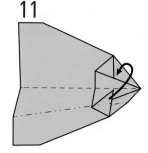

Close the model, while tucking the other corner into the same pocket to lock the fuselage.

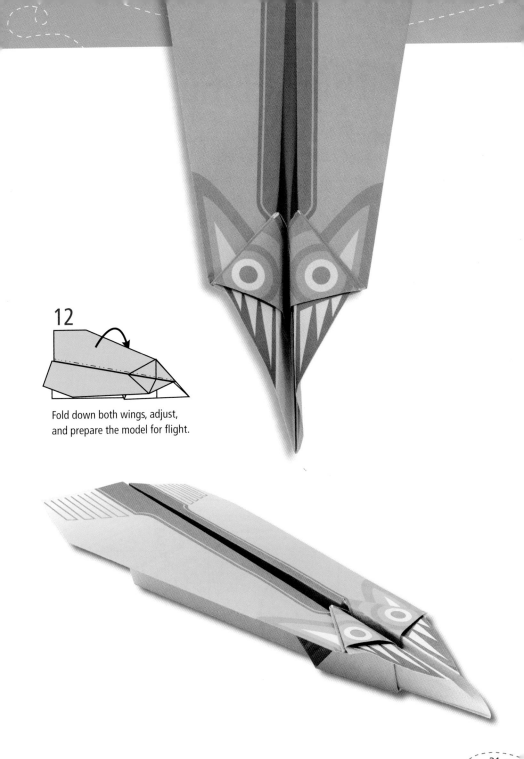

12

Fold down both wings, adjust,
and prepare the model for flight.

The Ladybug

By definition, all paper planes can be considered origami, in that they are folded from paper. Most familiar origami models are folded from squares, although folding from rectangles—currency in particular—has become very popular.

The reverse is true when it comes to paper planes. Most of us are completely unfamiliar with planes folded from squares. Everyone should learn this model. It is very simple and easy to fold, but it has effective weight distribution and flies beautifully. It even flies surprisingly well when folded from very small paper.

It is based on the "Sparrow" by the prolific paper airplane and origami designer, Nick Robinson.

Orientation

1

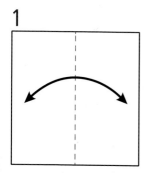

Begin with the printed side facing down. Valley fold through the center and unfold.

2

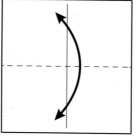

Valley fold through the center and unfold, top to bottom.

3

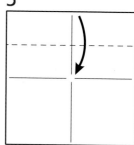

Valley fold the top edge to the horizontal crease.

4

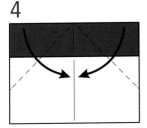

Make two valley folds, bringing the top edge down along both sides of the central crease.

5

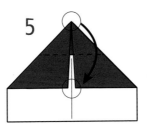

Valley fold the tip down to where the corner flaps intersect with the central crease.

6

Valley fold the tip up, so that it reaches just above the top edge.

7

Mountain fold in half.

Rotate 90 degrees.

8

Fold the wings down to meet the bottom edge.

9

Adjust and prepare the model for flight.

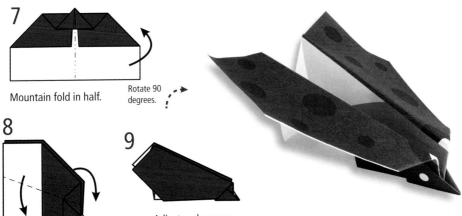

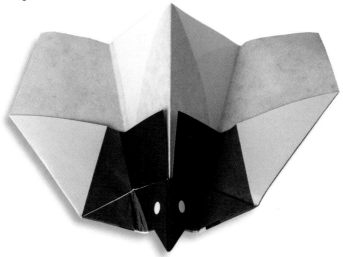

The Lock Wing Glider

This well-balanced glider flies reliably and gracefully, thanks to its large, sturdy wings. It should be thrown with moderate force, with the wings set at a positive dihedral (Y shape). If the plane dives, fold the trailing edges of the wings up slightly. This is a good model for tricks and circular flight. It possesses landing gear, near its nose, which changes the nature of its flight when deployed. You can also lock the front and/or back if desired.

Orientation

1

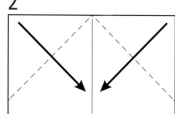

Begin with the unprinted side facing up, with the long sides oriented horizontally. Valley fold through the center and unfold.

2

Fold the top edges to the central crease.

3

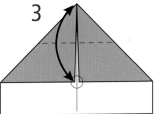

Valley fold the tip down to the corners of the uppermost flaps. Unfold.

4

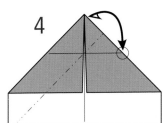

Mountain fold the tip down to the right edge of the crease you just made. Unfold.

5

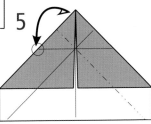

Repeat on the other side.

6

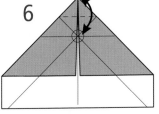

Valley fold and unfold the top corner to the intersection.

7

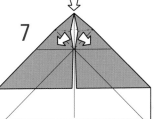

Pull out the corners and squash fold them down.

8

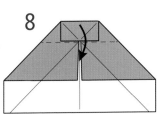

Valley fold from the base of the rectangle.

9

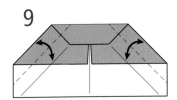

Valley fold the diagonal edges down to the creases. Unfold.

10

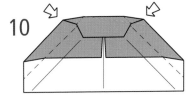

Inside reverse fold the two diagonal edges along the creases you just made.

11

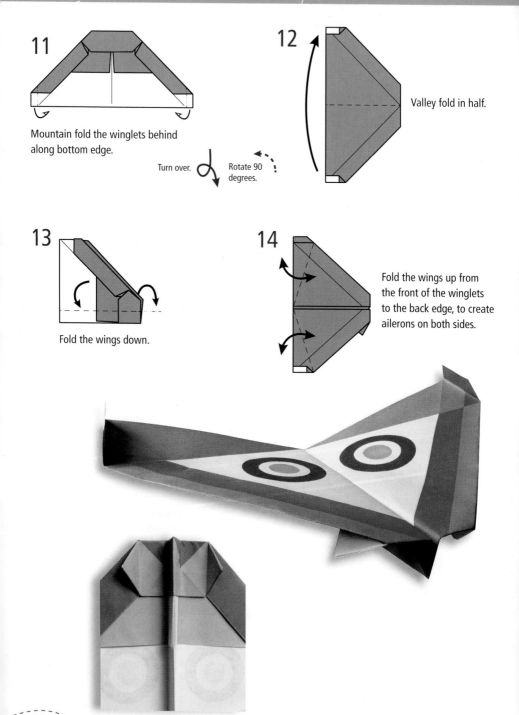

Mountain fold the winglets behind along bottom edge.

Turn over.

Rotate 90 degrees.

12

Valley fold in half.

13

Fold the wings down.

14

Fold the wings up from the front of the winglets to the back edge, to create ailerons on both sides.

The Martian Cruiser

Planes from square paper do not necessarily fly any better than those from rectangles. It does open a whole new range of possibilities for planes, though. Particularly from a diagonal orientation. Square-based models can be folded from typical origami paper (*kami*). Kami is very thin and light. It is strong and folds well in all directions. These properties are all excellent for folding planes to be flown indoors. The square format allows for the eccentric shape of the Martian Cruiser. Its design was inspired by mid-twentieth century science fiction.

Orientation

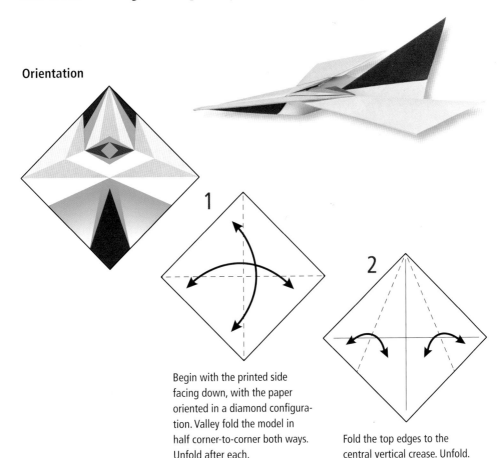

1

Begin with the printed side facing down, with the paper oriented in a diamond configuration. Valley fold the model in half corner-to-corner both ways. Unfold after each.

2

Fold the top edges to the central vertical crease. Unfold.

3

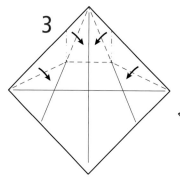

Valley fold the top halves of the diagonal edges to the vertical center, and the bottom halves to the horizontal center. This will form a triangle at the top of the model. See the next diagram for the shape.

4

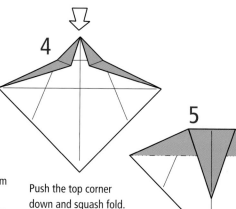

Push the top corner down and squash fold.

5

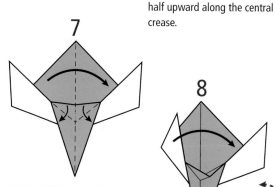

Mountain fold the bottom half upward along the central crease.

6

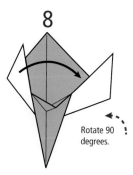

Valley fold the wings upward, completing the creases under the triangular flap.

7

Valley fold the model in half, pulling the top edge of the triangular flap down as you do so.

8

Rotate 90 degrees.

Continue folding the model in half.

9

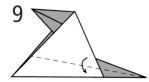

Fold the wing down, bisecting the nose of the plane

10

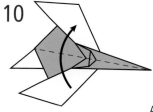

Unfold.

11

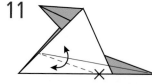

At point x, the plane becomes thicker. Fold from point x to the intersection of the edge and the crease.

12

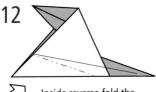

Inside reverse fold the corner along the crease.

13

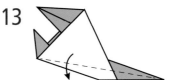

Fold the wing down.

14

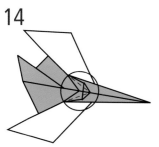

Zoom in on the fuselage.

15

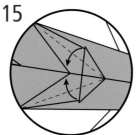

Valley fold the tips of the flaps down as far as they will go.

16

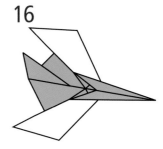

Straighten the fuselage, adjust, and prepare the model for flight.

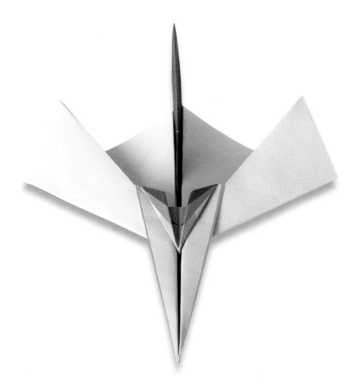

The Martian Fighter

Another Martian aircraft, this one is built for speed. Taking full advantage of possibilities offered by the square format, in flight it resembles a dart, a great deal more than "The Dart." Just take care not to hit anyone's eye with its extremely pointy nose. The wings and fuselage lock nicely, while the tail can hang open a bit, giving the plane more gliding ability.

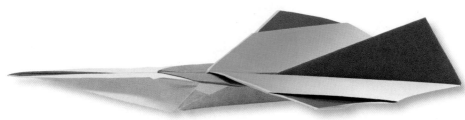

Orientation

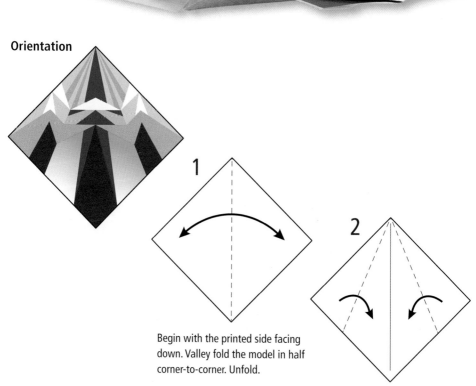

1

Begin with the printed side facing down. Valley fold the model in half corner-to-corner. Unfold.

2

Fold the top edges to the central crease.

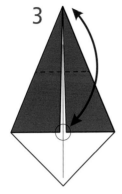

3

Fold the tip down to where the corner flaps intersect with the central crease. Unfold.

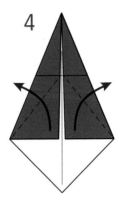

4

Valley fold the two corners up diagonally, using the crease you just made as a guide.

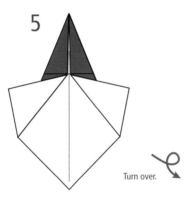

5

Turn over.

The result.

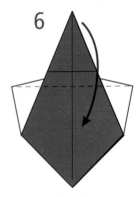

6

Valley fold the tip down along the greatest width.

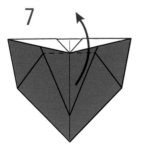

7

Refold nose upward along the existing crease.

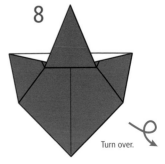

8

Turn over.

The result.

9

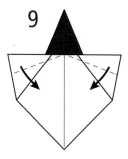

Valley fold the edges of the wings downward from the center point, as far as they will go.

10

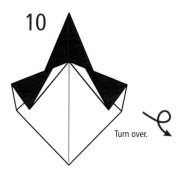

Turn over.

The result.

11

Valley fold the model in half, bringing the base of the triangular flap up as far as it will go.

12

Step 11 in progress.

13

Valley fold the wing flap over and down so that the top edge almost lies even with the left side of the model.

14

Unfold.

15

Valley fold to form the tail fin. Unfold.

16

Inside reverse fold along the crease you just made.

17

Fold the wing down.

18

The result.

Turn over.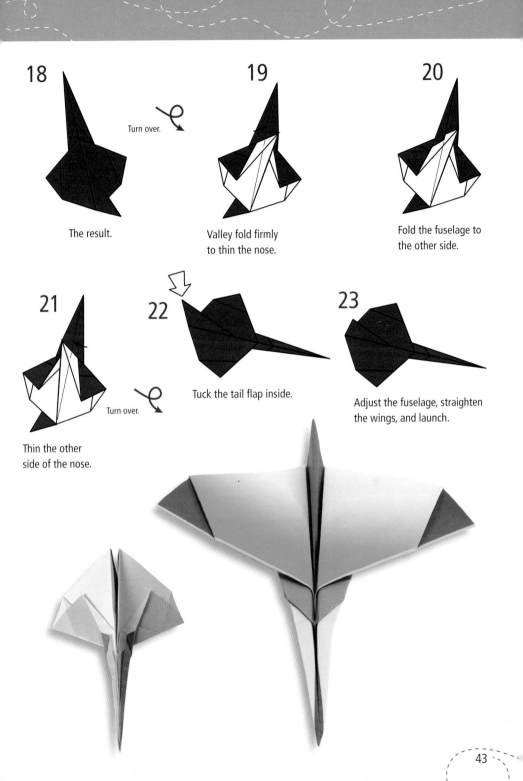

19

Valley fold firmly
to thin the nose.

20

Fold the fuselage to
the other side.

21

Turn over.

Thin the other
side of the nose.

22

Tuck the tail flap inside.

23

Adjust the fuselage, straighten
the wings, and launch.

The UFO

This model was inspired by elements of Edo period Japanese origami. It is meant to be thrown high, spinning like a frisbee. It makes for a much less destructive indoor toy. Being relatively durable, and lacking a point, it is good for younger children to play with. Throw it at a steep enough angle and it will come back to you.

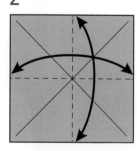

Orientation

1

Begin with the printed side facing up. Valley fold and unfold, corner-to-corner, both ways, leaving a crease in the shape of an X down the center.

2

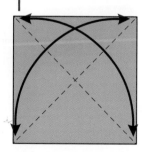

Fold and unfold top to bottom and side to side.

3

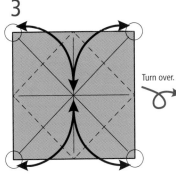

Fold all four corners to the center. Unfold.

Turn over.

4

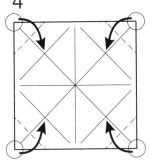

Fold the corners to the intersections.

5

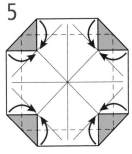

Fold in all the edges, so that the outside edges meet the folded, inside corners.

6

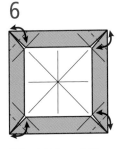

Valley fold the outside corners to meet the inside corners. Unfold.

7

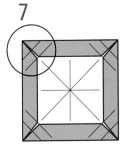

Zoom in on the corner.

8

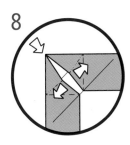

Pull out the corners and squash fold the tip down.

9

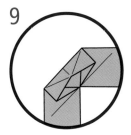

Squash fold flat. Zoom out.

10

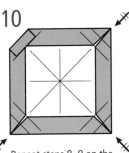

Repeat steps 8–9 on the other three corners.

11

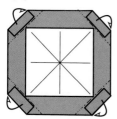

Firmly mountain fold the
four corners behind along
the existing creases.

12

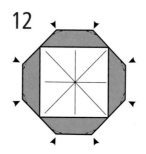

Mountain fold all of the
corners downward to
round the disc.

About the Author

Sam Ita lives in Queens, New York. Having studied graphic design at the Pratt Institute in Brooklyn, he began working as a paper engineer and creating pop-up books. Taking his inspiration from comics, origami, and various other sources, he has applied his talents to publishing, advertising, animation, and toy design. He is noted for his pop-up adaptations of such famous novels as *Moby Dick*, *20,000 Leagues Under the Sea*, *Frankenstein,* and *The Odyssey*.

Published in 2016 by Tuttle Publishing, an imprint of Periplus Editions (HK) Ltd.

www.tuttlepublishing.com

Original edition:
Aerei di Carta © 2015 Nuinui
www.nuinui.ch
Nuinui is an imprint of Snake SA, Switzerland

Editorial director: Federica Romagnoli
Art director and graphic design: Clara Zanotti
Editorial assistant: Diana Bertinetti

ISBN 978-0-8048-4609-7

English Translation © 2016 Periplus Editions (HK) Ltd.

Distributed by
North America, Latin America & Europe
Tuttle Publishing
364 Innovation Drive, North Clarendon,
VT 05759-9436 U.S.A.
Tel: (802) 773-8930
Fax: (802) 773-6993
info@tuttlepublishing.com
www.tuttlepublishing.com

Asia Pacific
Berkeley Books Pte. Ltd.
61 Tai Seng Avenue #02-12, Singapore 534167
Tel: (65) 6280-1330
Fax: (65) 6280-6290
inquiries@periplus.com.sg
www.periplus.com

Printed in China   1605VP
19 18 17 16   6 5 4 3 2

TUTTLE PUBLISHING® is a registered trademark of Tuttle Publishing, a division of Periplus Editions (HK) Ltd.

About Tuttle
"Books to Span the East and West"

Our core mission at Tuttle Publishing is to create books which bring people together one page at a time. Tuttle was founded in 1832 in the small New England town of Rutland, Vermont (USA). Our fundamental values remain as strong today as they were then—to publish best-in-class books informing the English-speaking world about the countries and peoples of Asia. The world has become a smaller place today and Asia's economic, cultural and political influence has expanded, yet the need for meaningful dialogue and information about this diverse region has never been greater. Since 1948, Tuttle has been a leader in publishing books on the cultures, arts, cuisines, languages and literatures of Asia. Our authors and photographers have won numerous awards and Tuttle has published thousands of books on subjects ranging from martial arts to paper crafts. We welcome you to explore the wealth of information available on Asia at **www.tuttlepublishing.com**.